I0463623

About

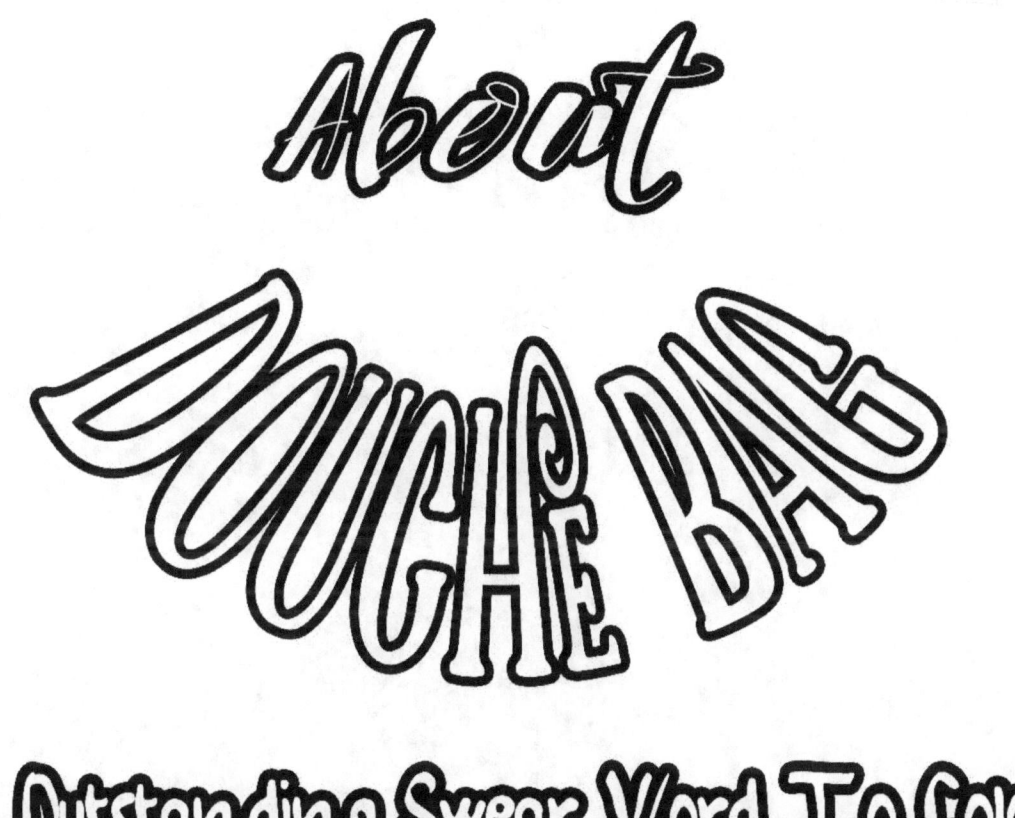

DOUCHE BAG

Outstanding Swear Word To Color

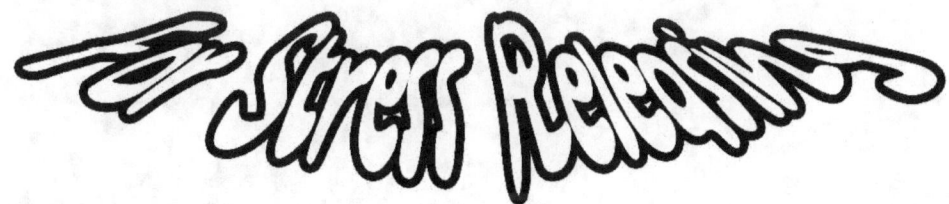

For Stress Releasing

Jo Millie Nawthorn

Copyright © 2017 by JA Millie Hawthorn

All rights reserved worldwide. No part of this publication may be reproduced or distributed in any form or by any means, mechanical, electronic or stored in a retrieval or database system, without written permission from the copyright holder.

Happy Coloring!

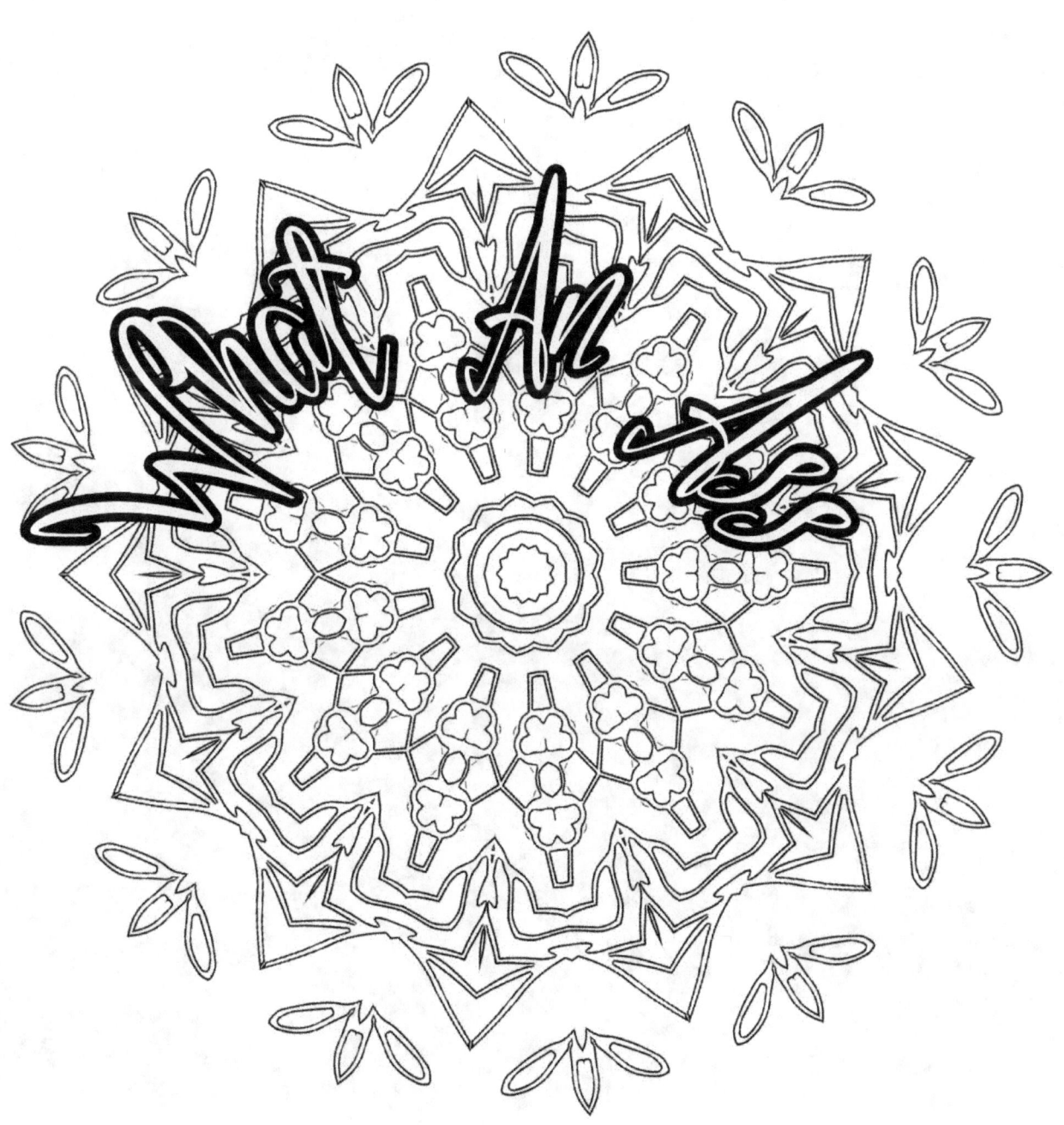

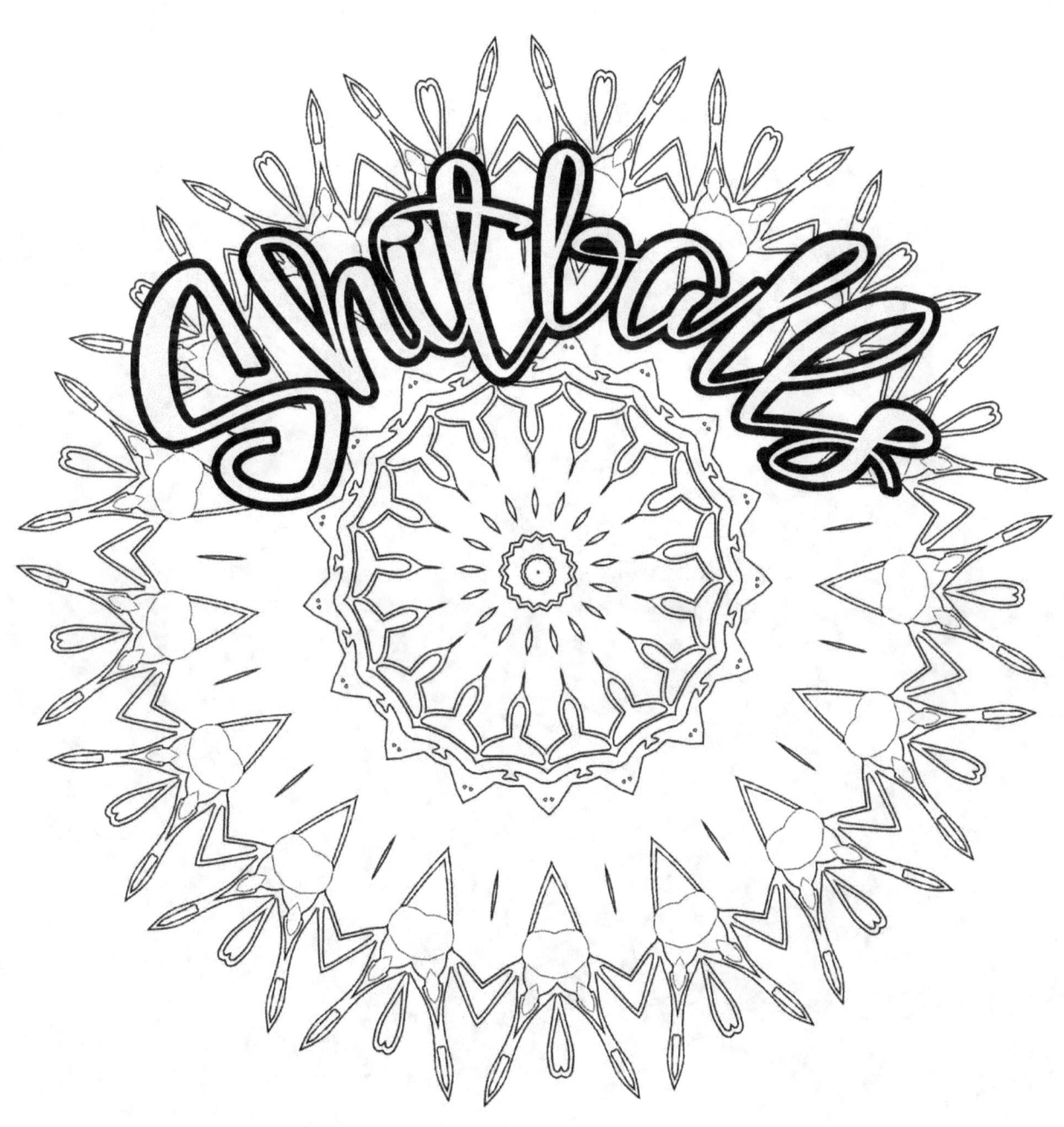

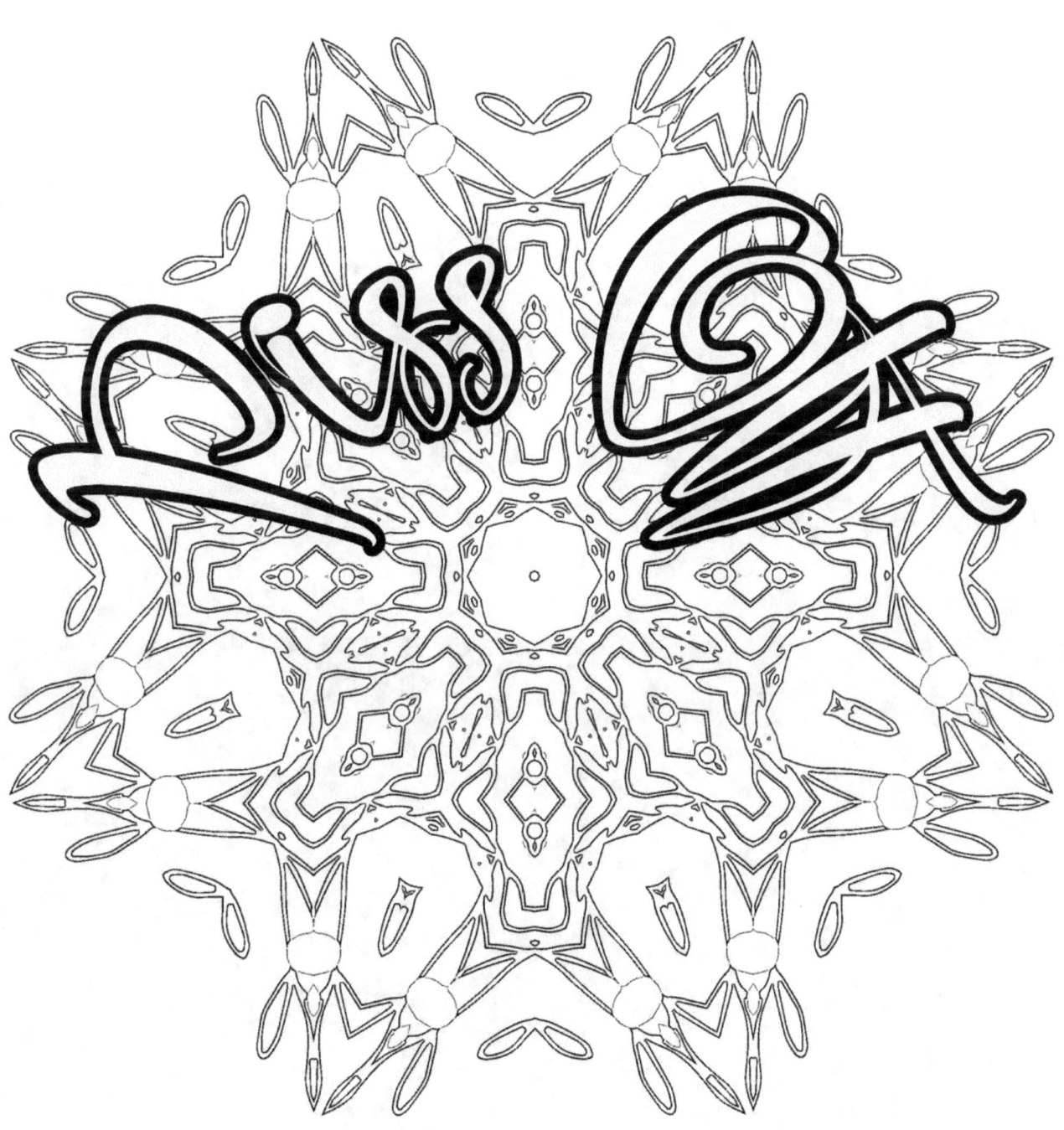

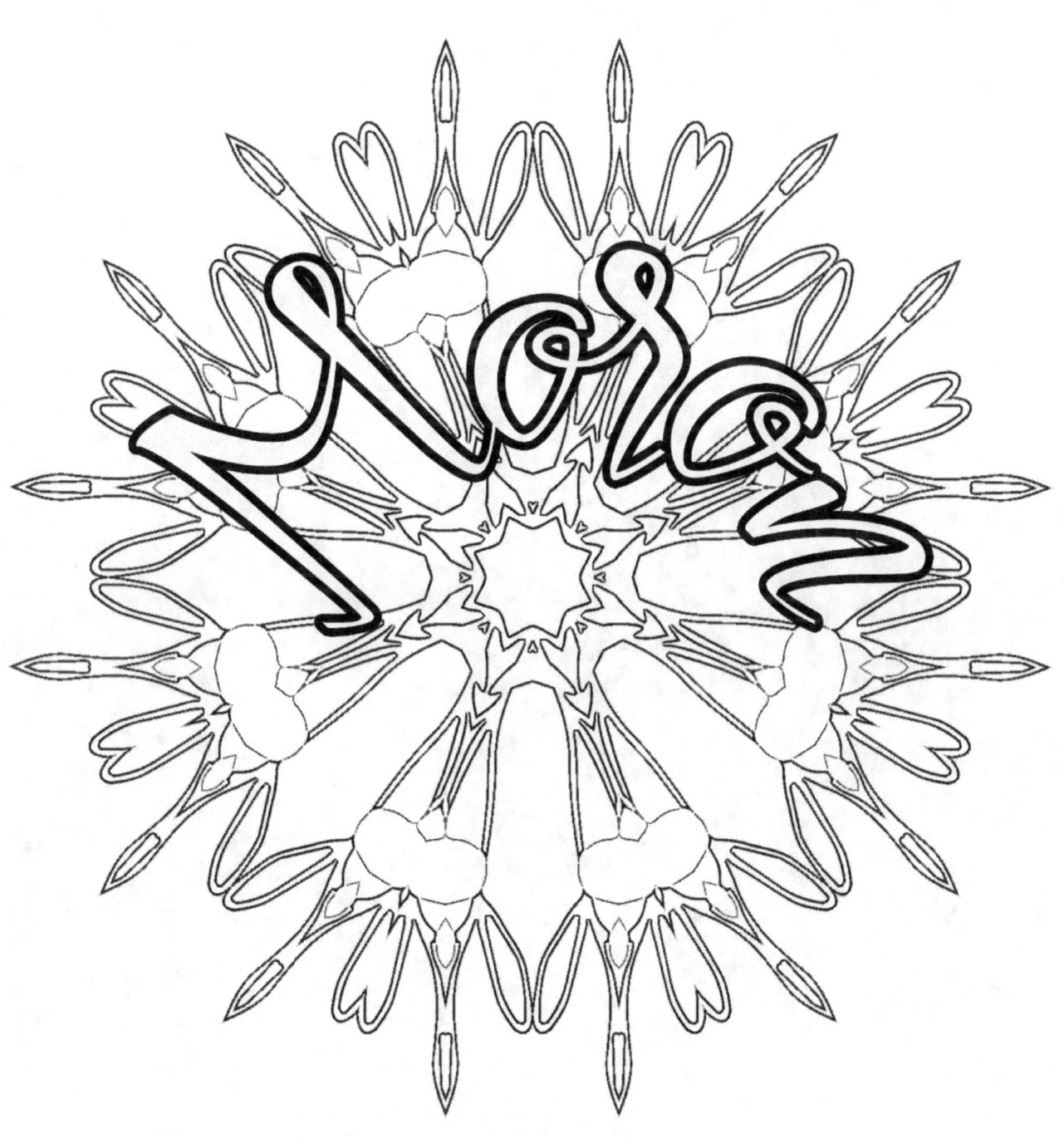

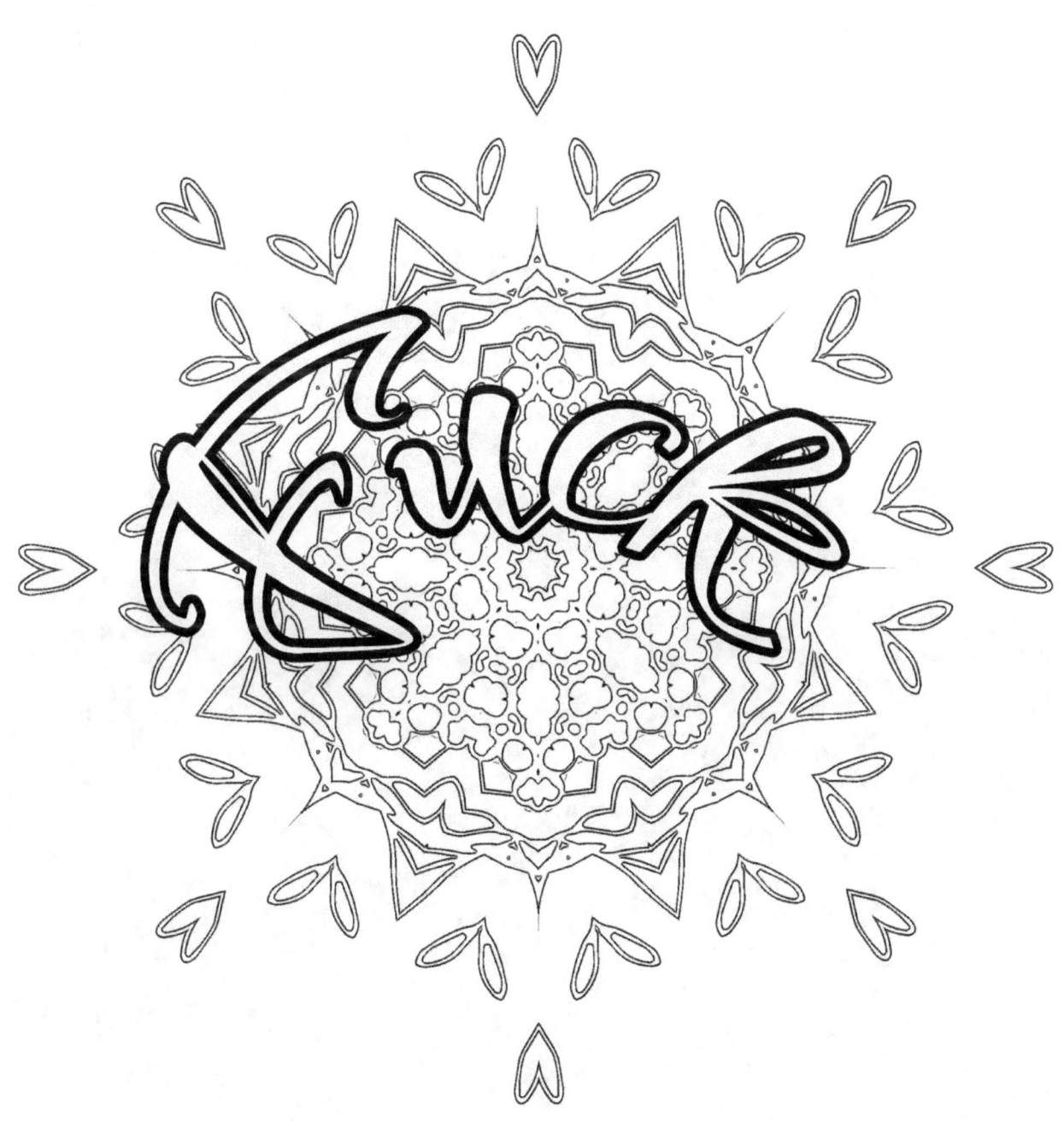

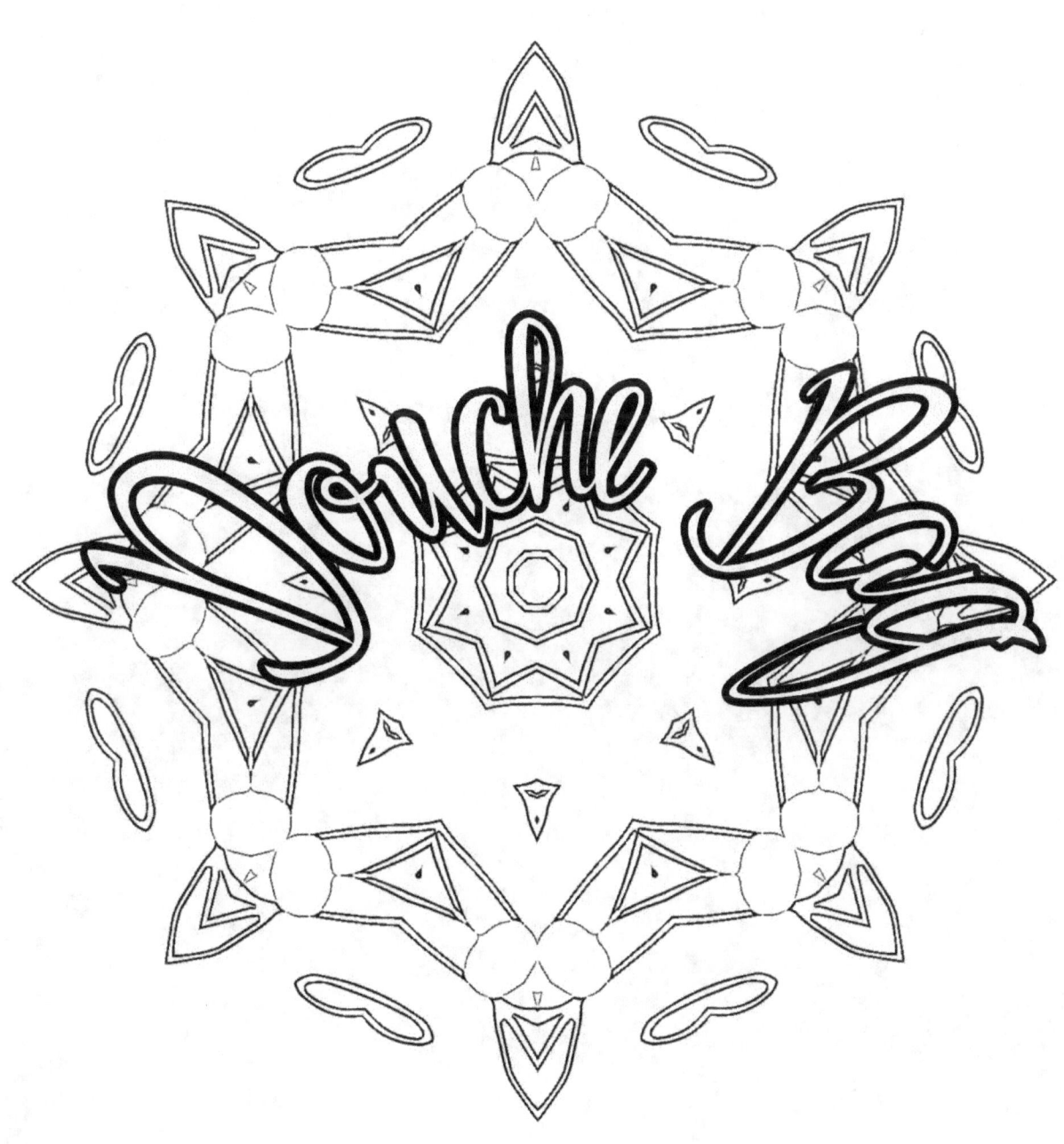

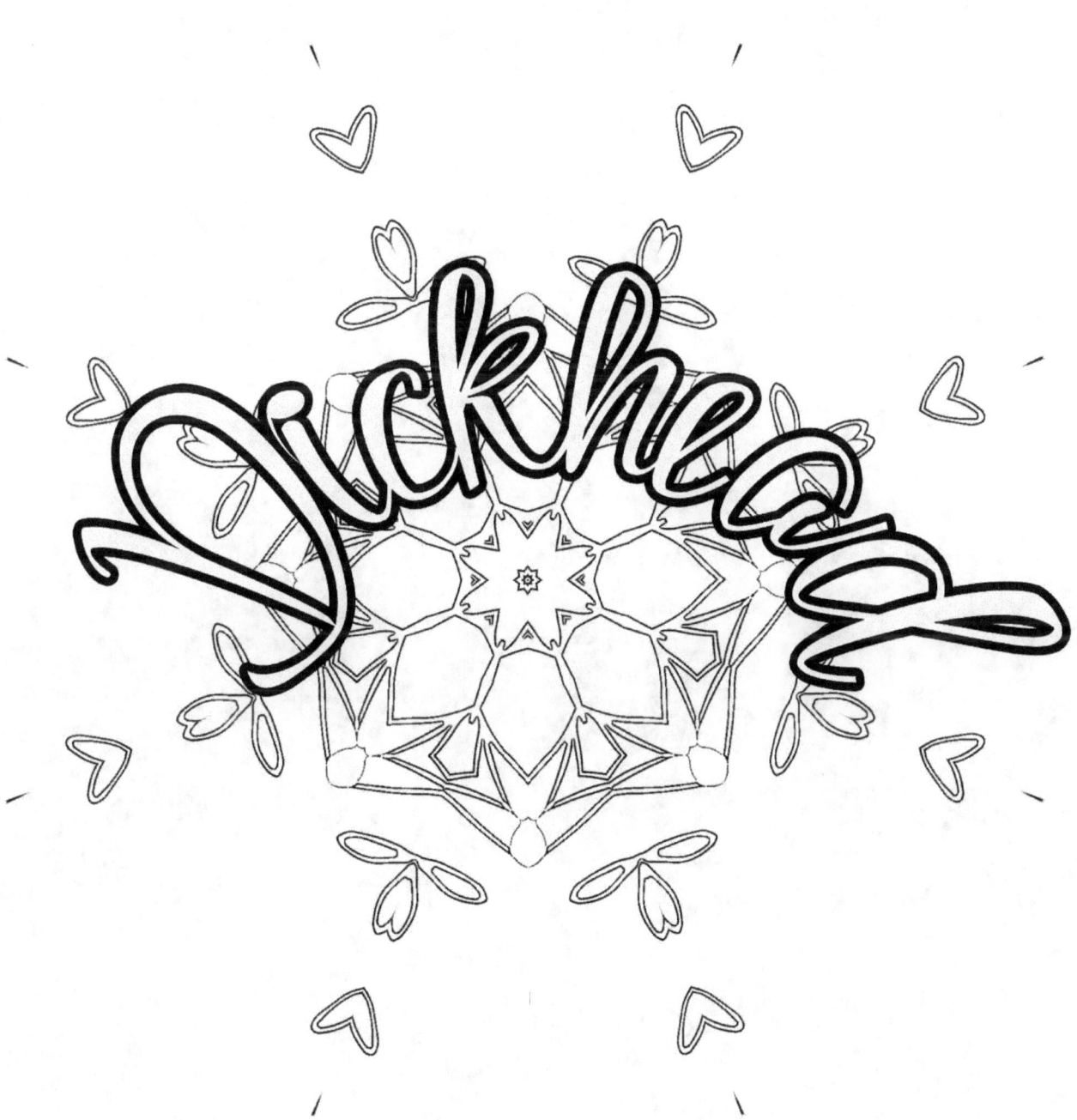

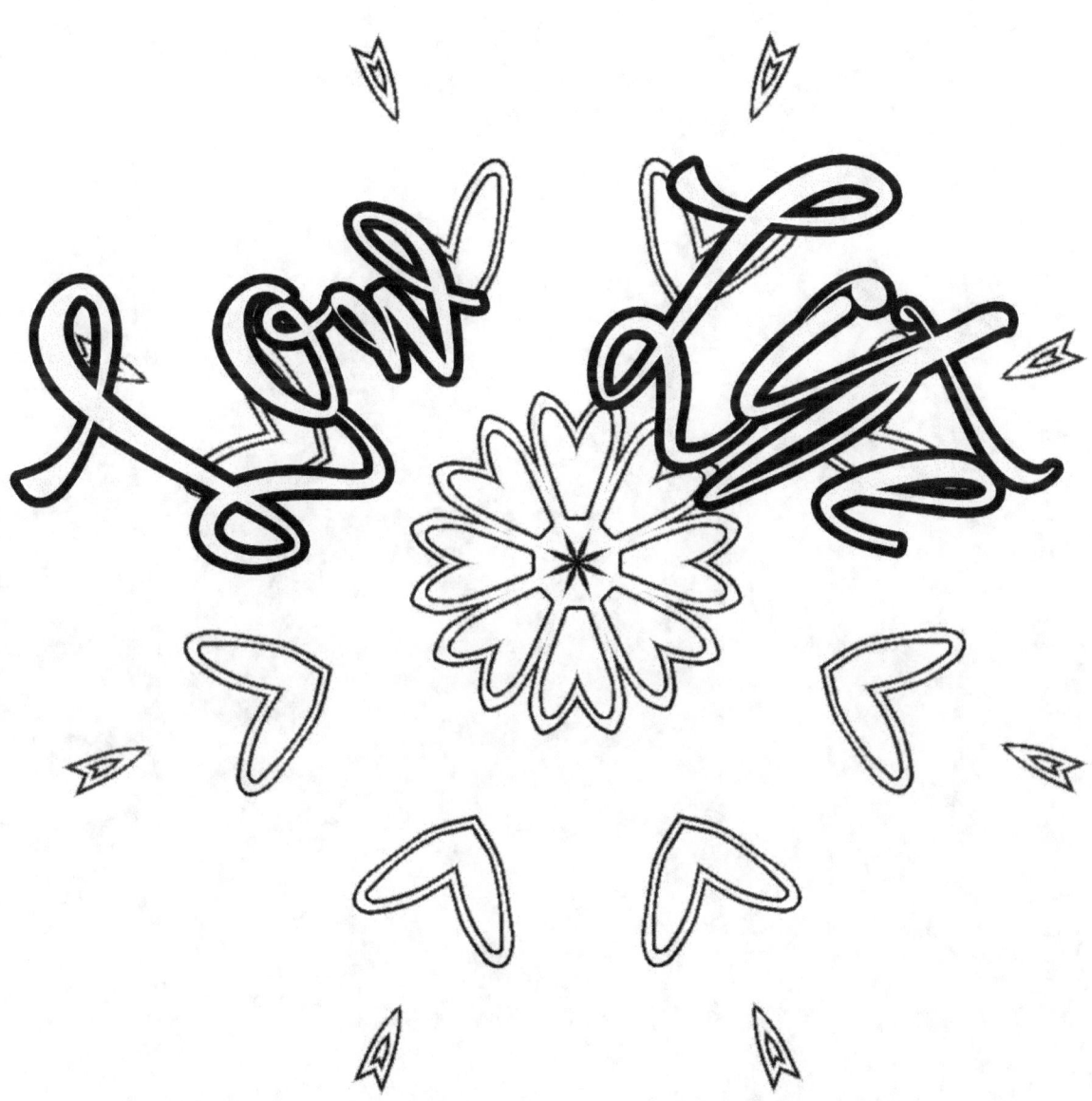

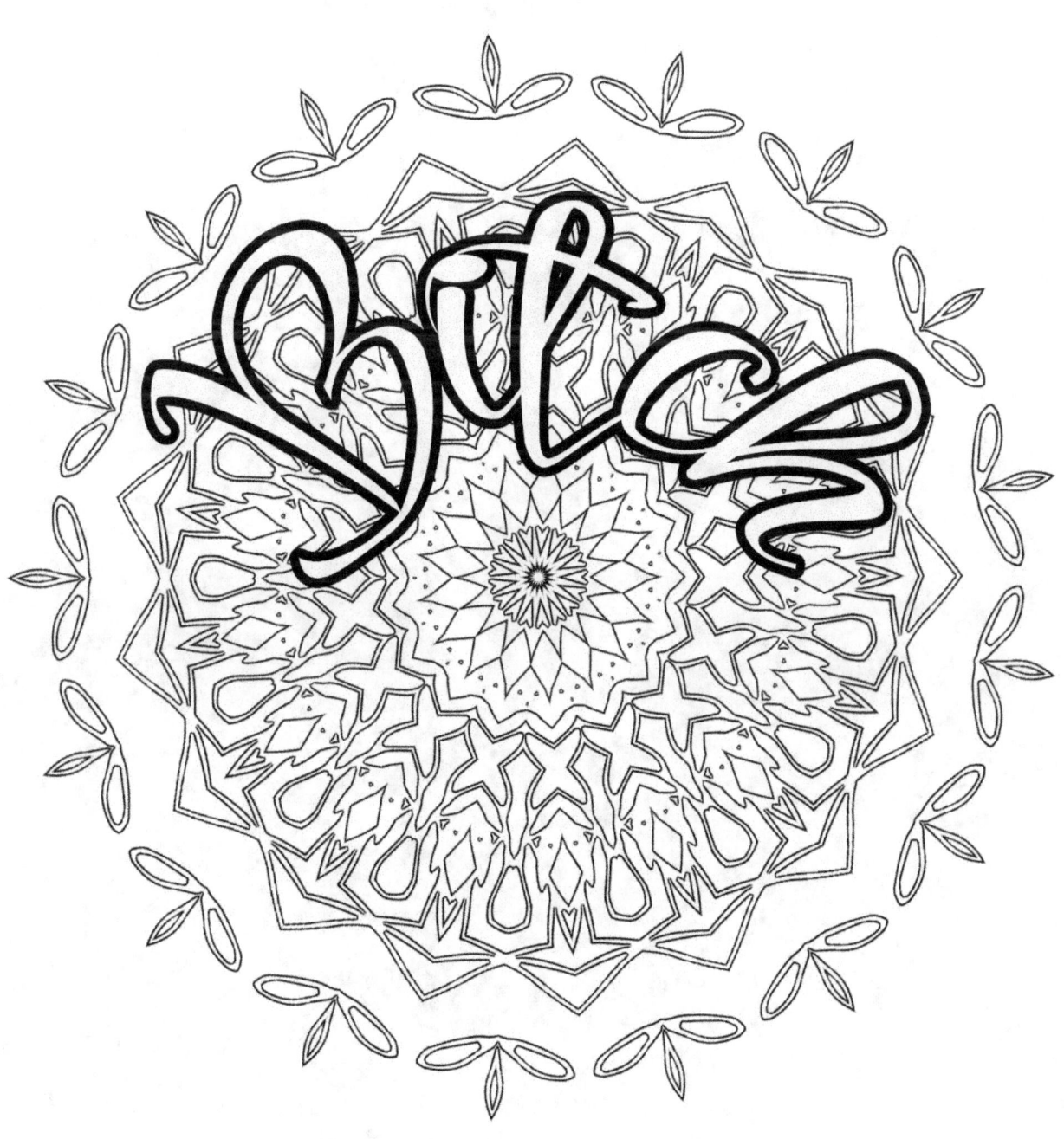

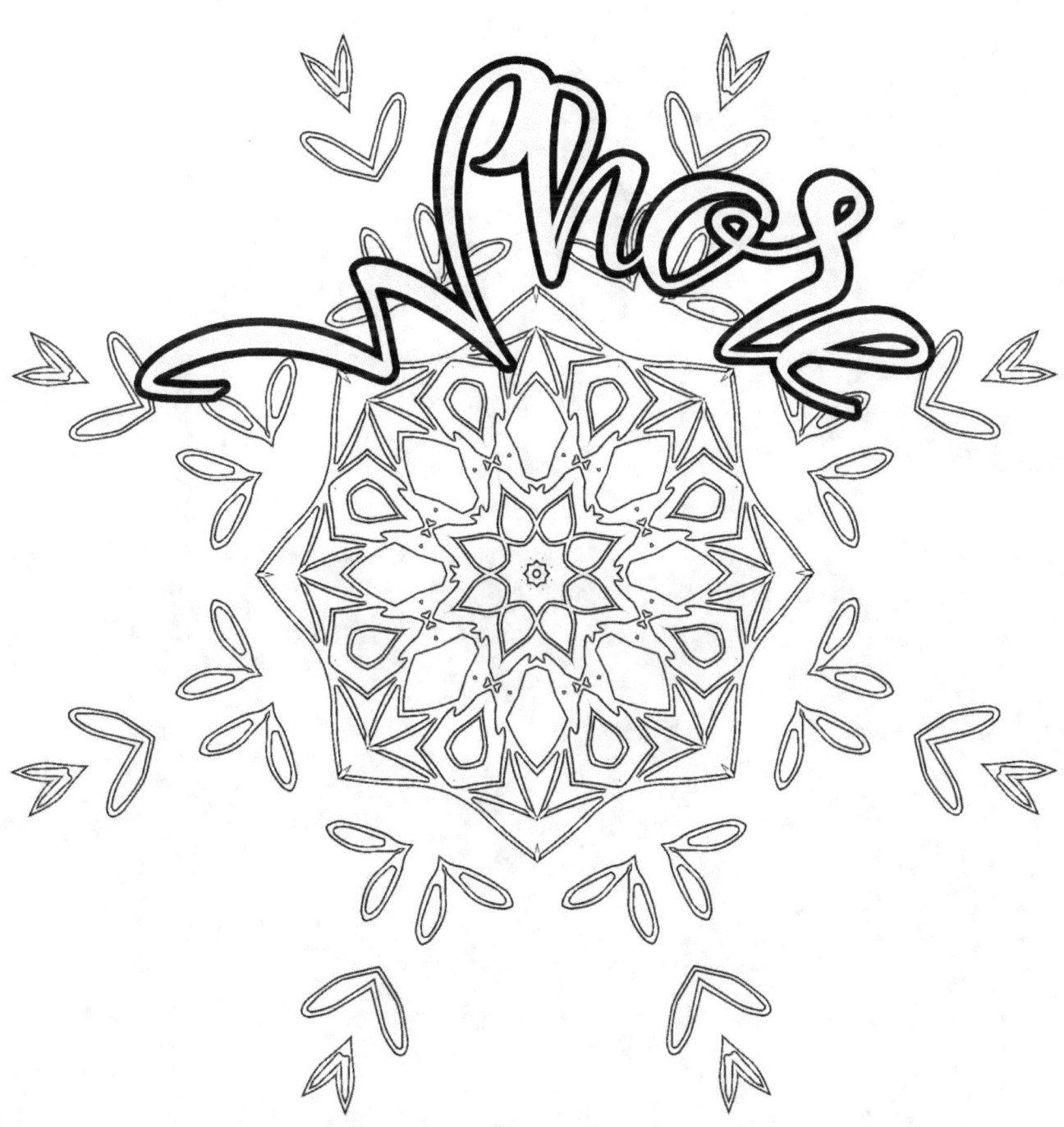

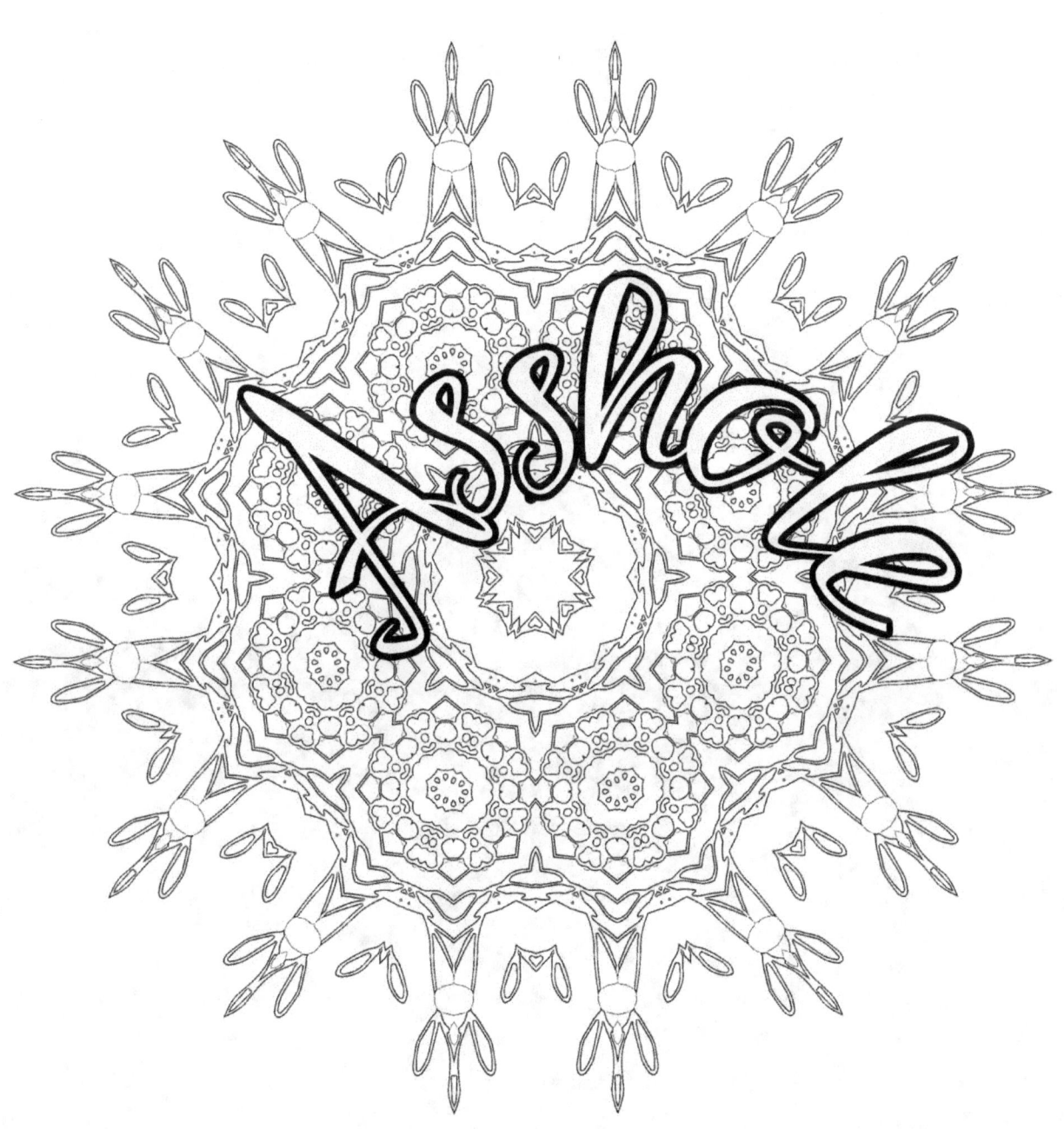

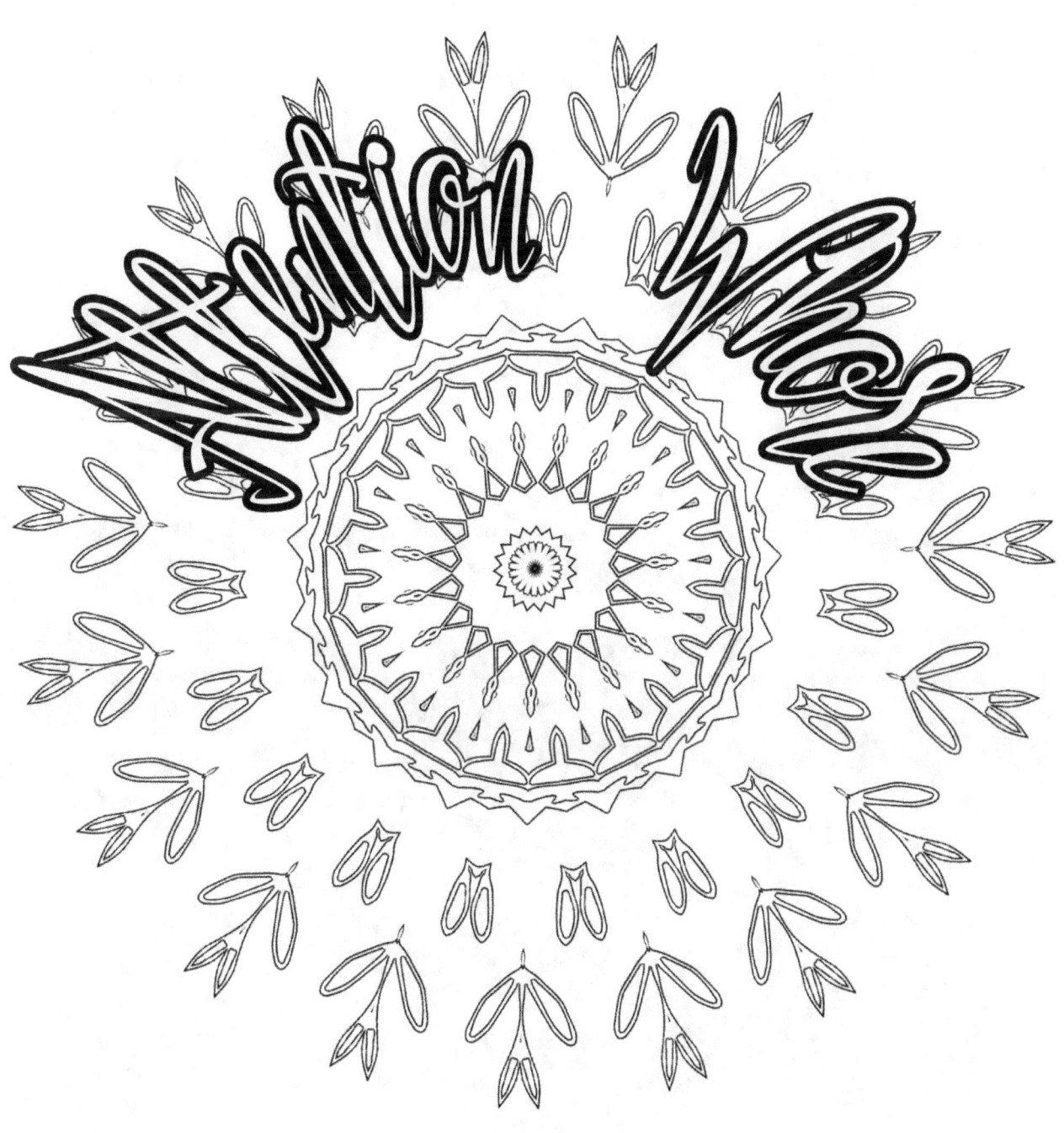

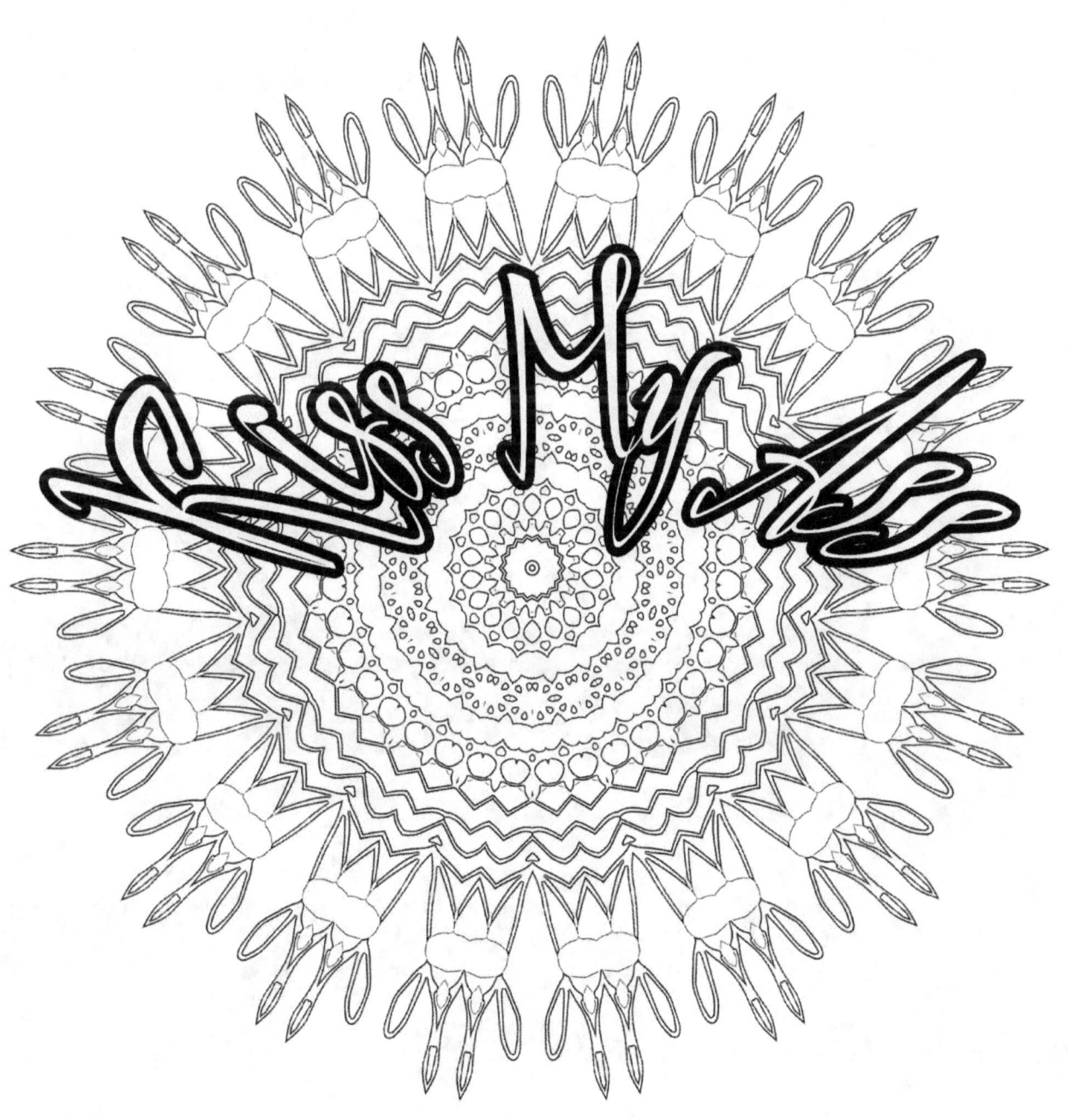

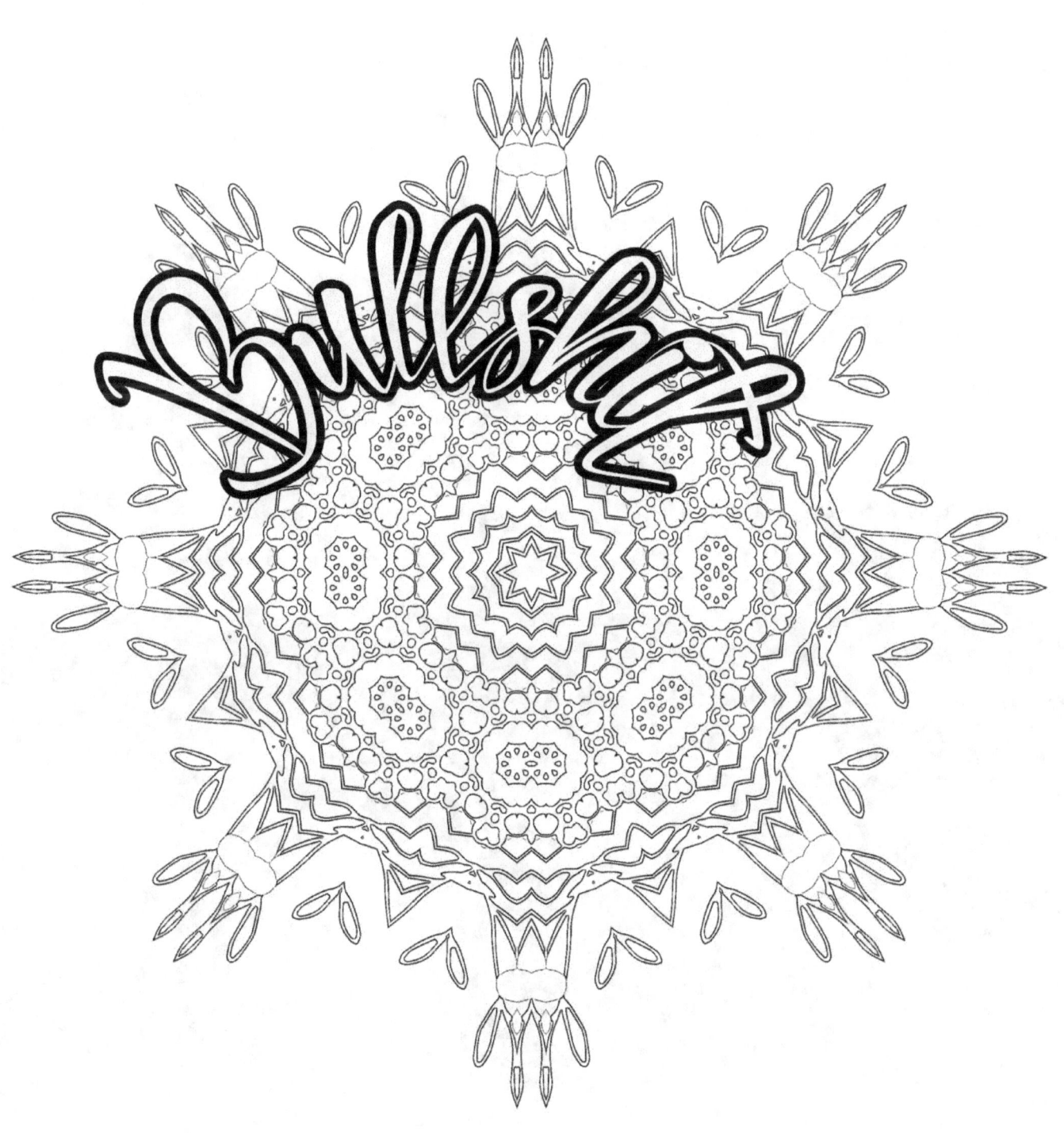

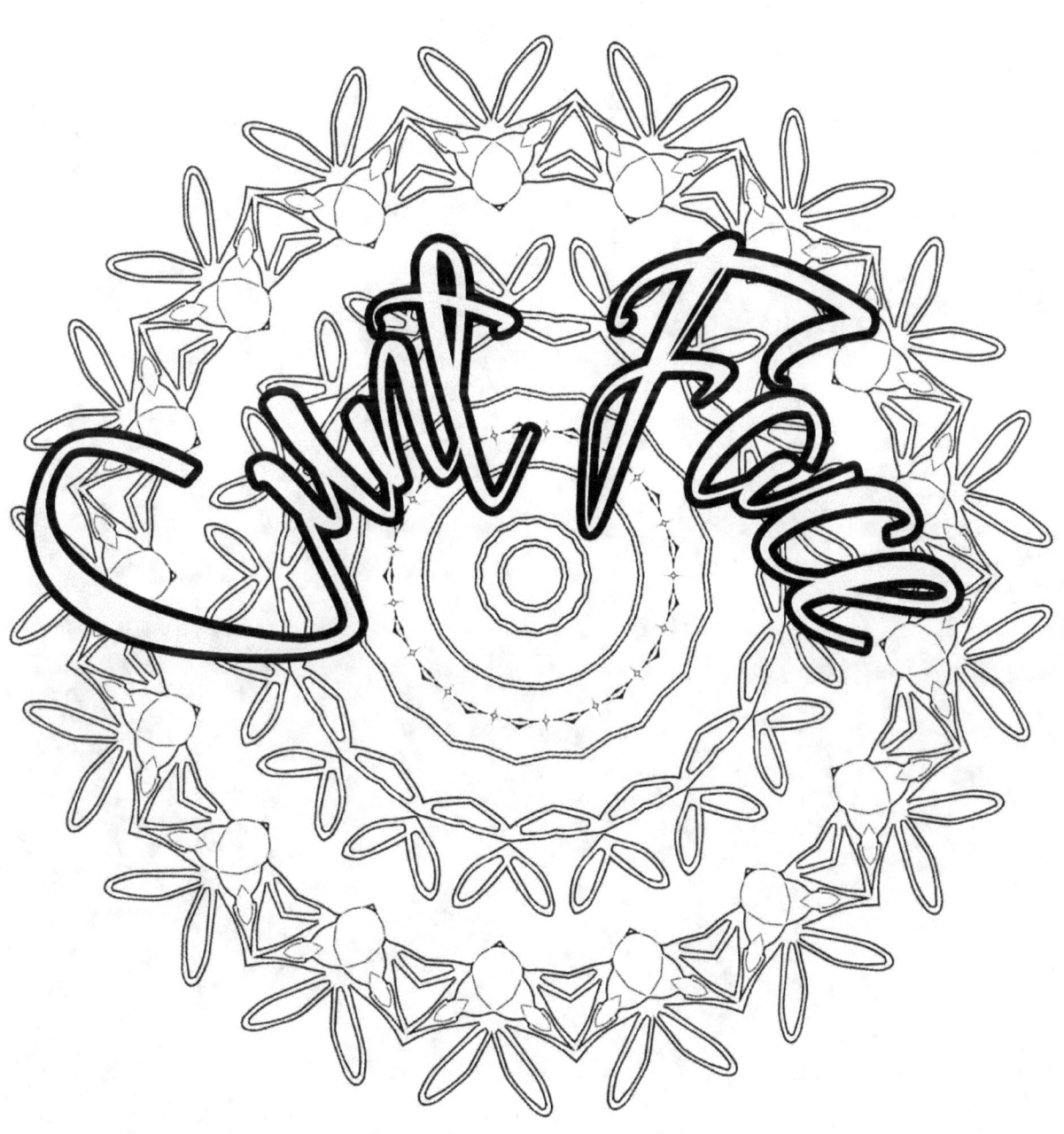

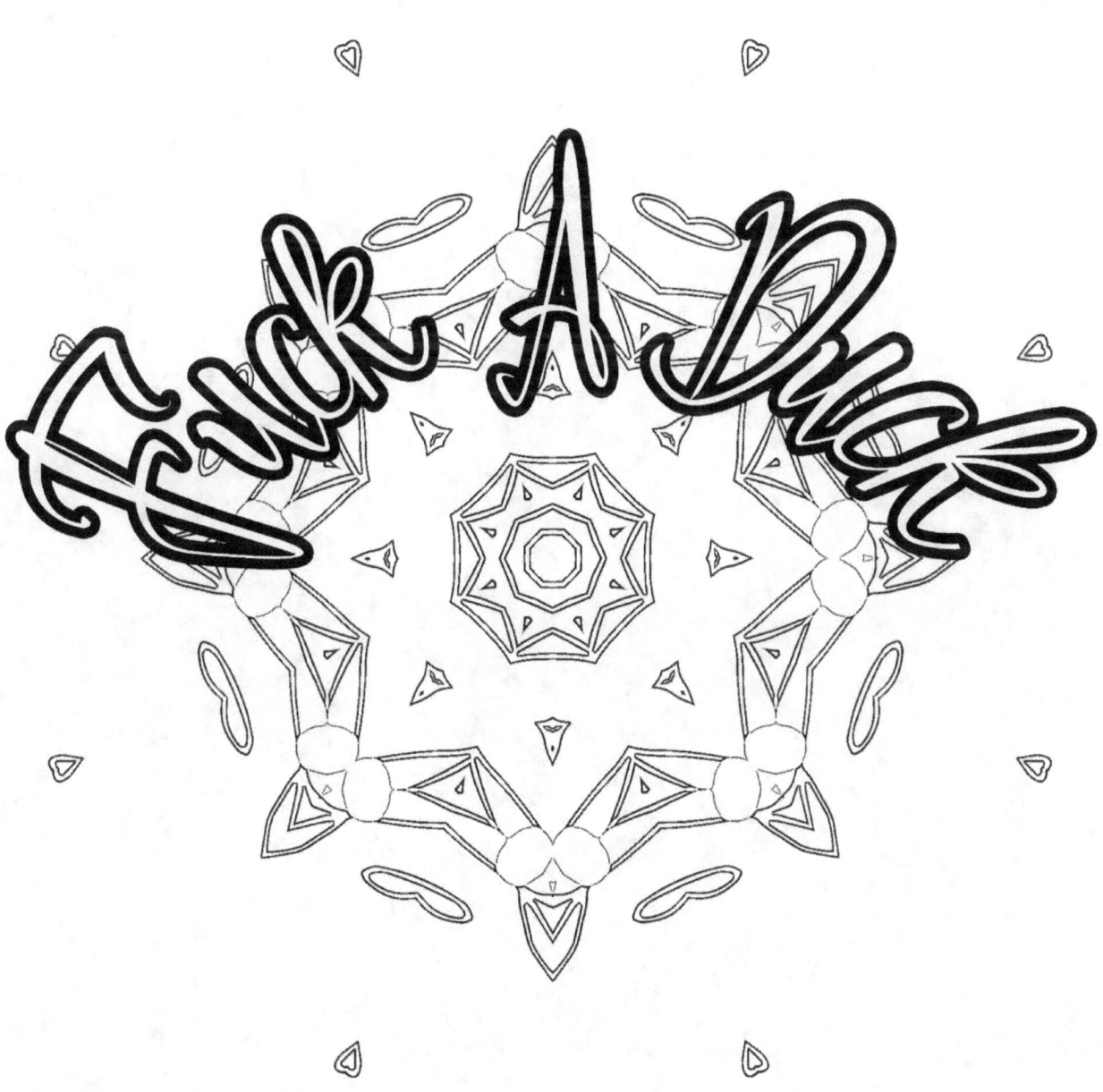

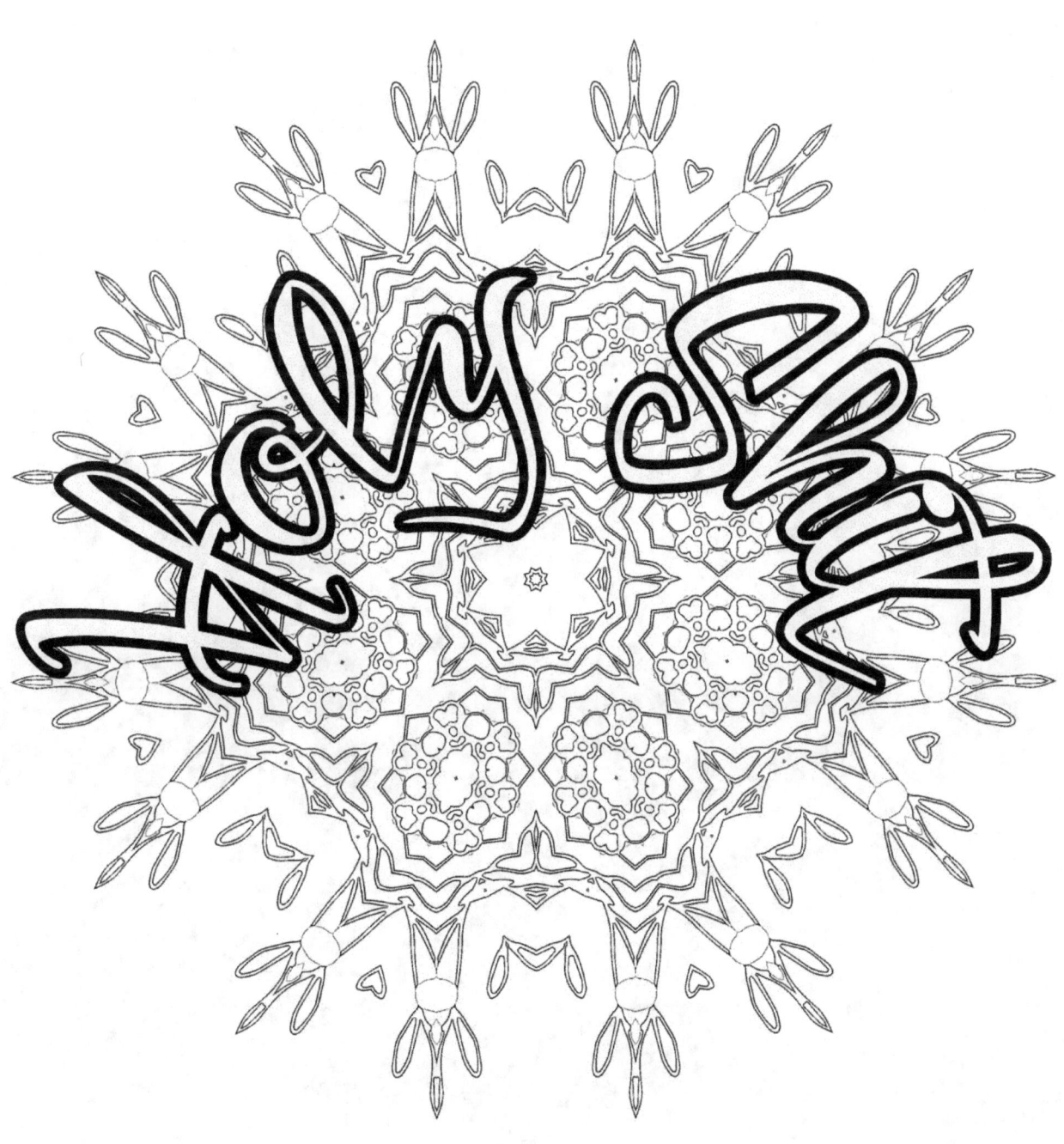

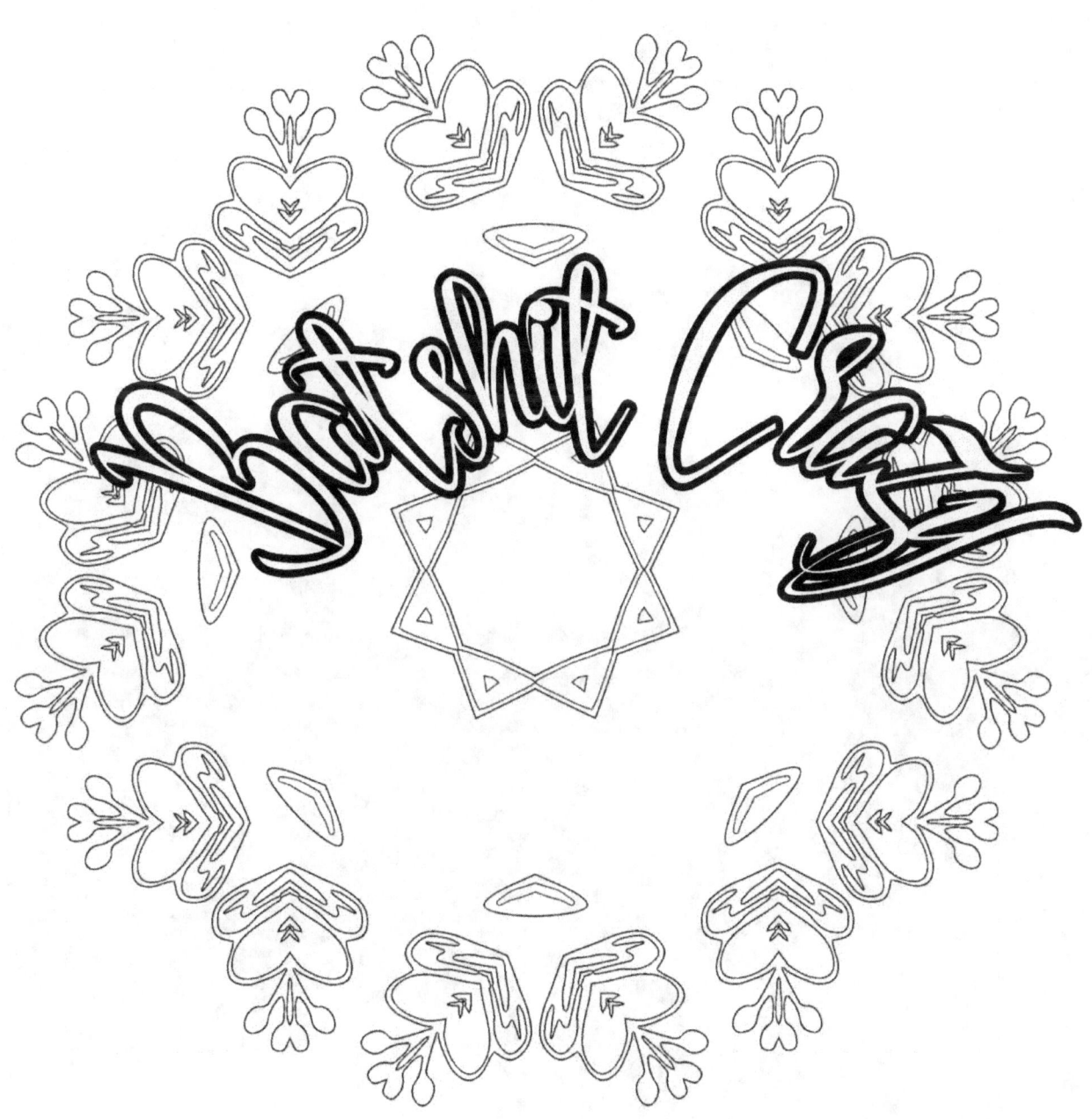

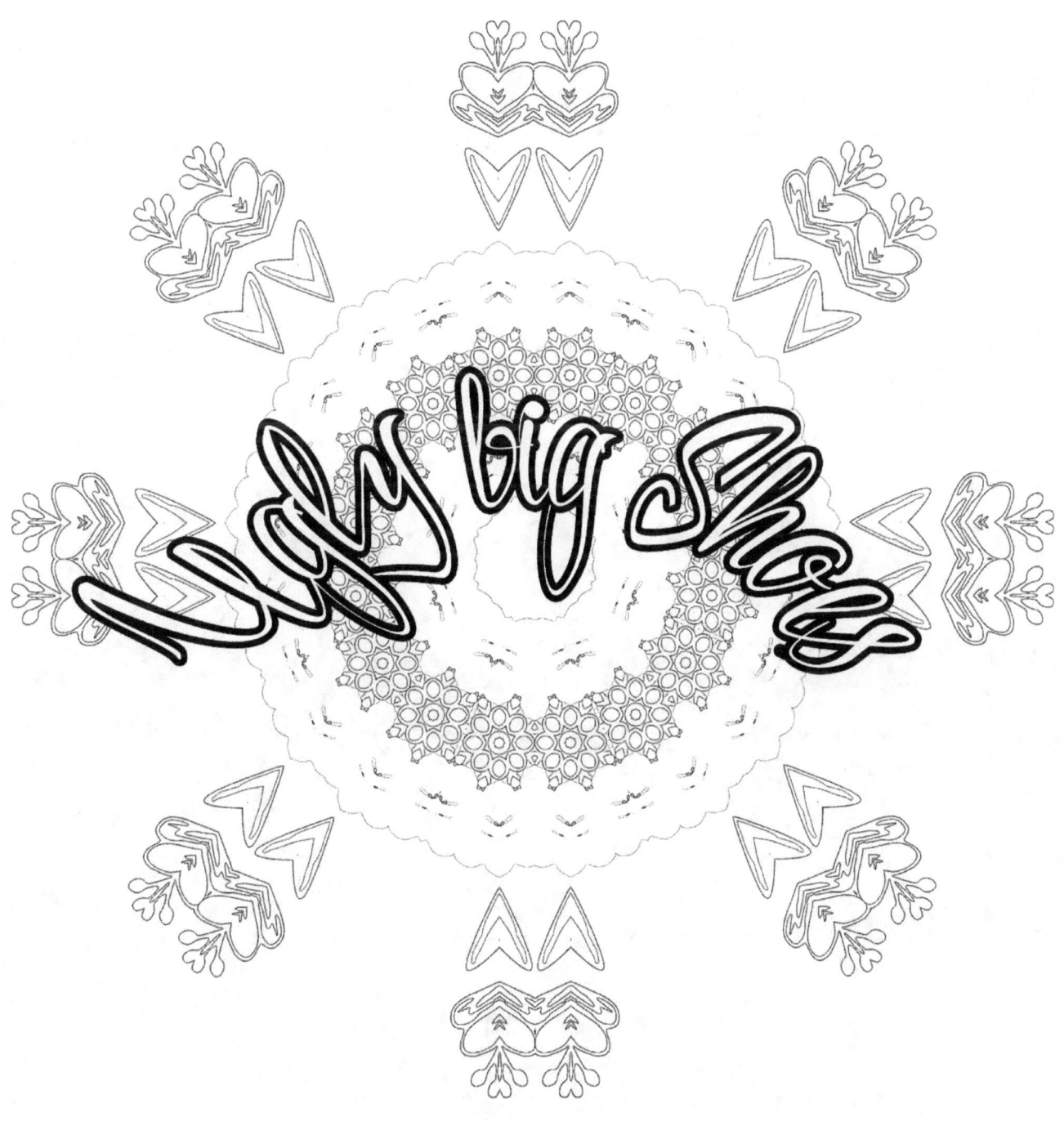

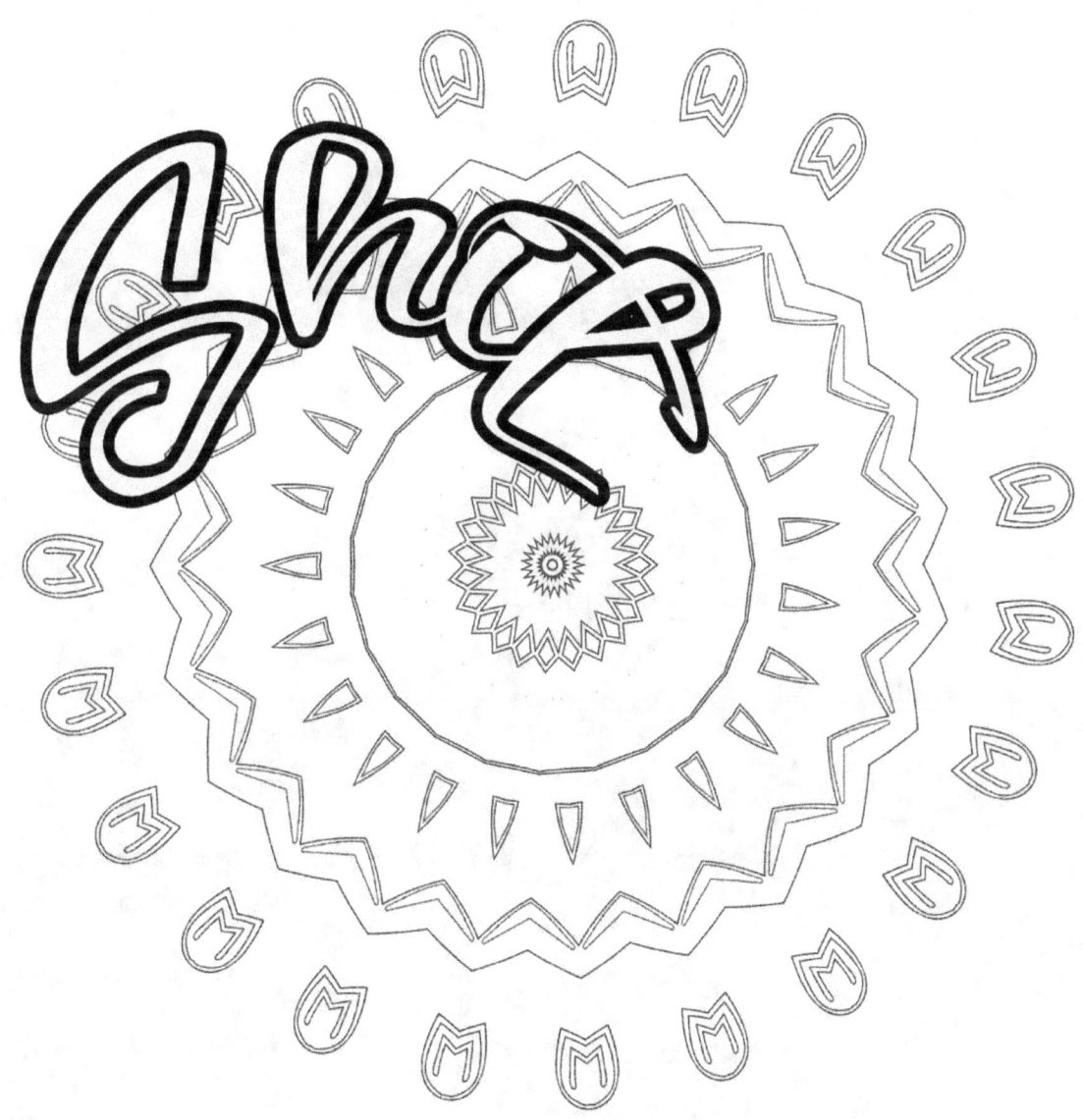

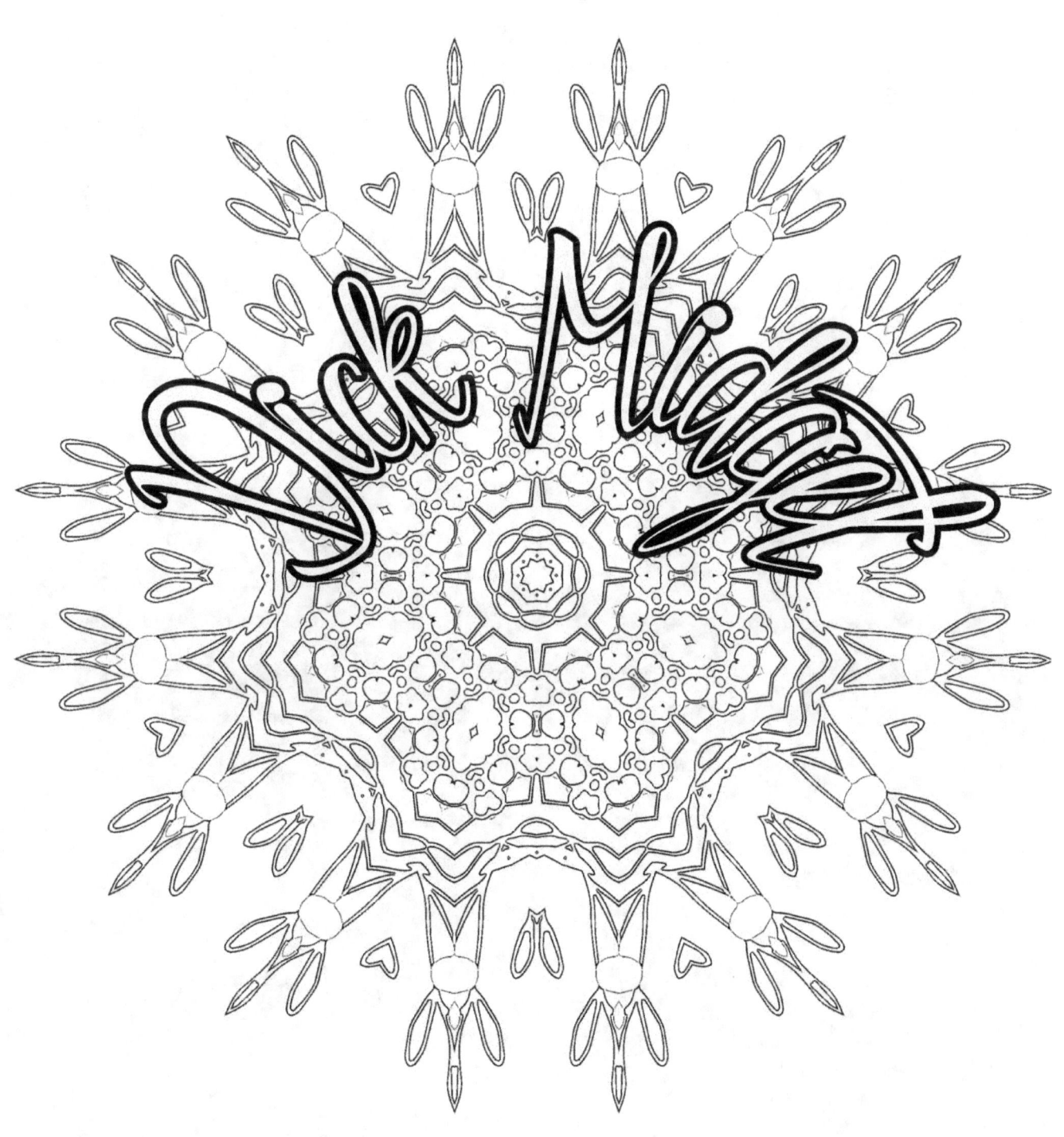

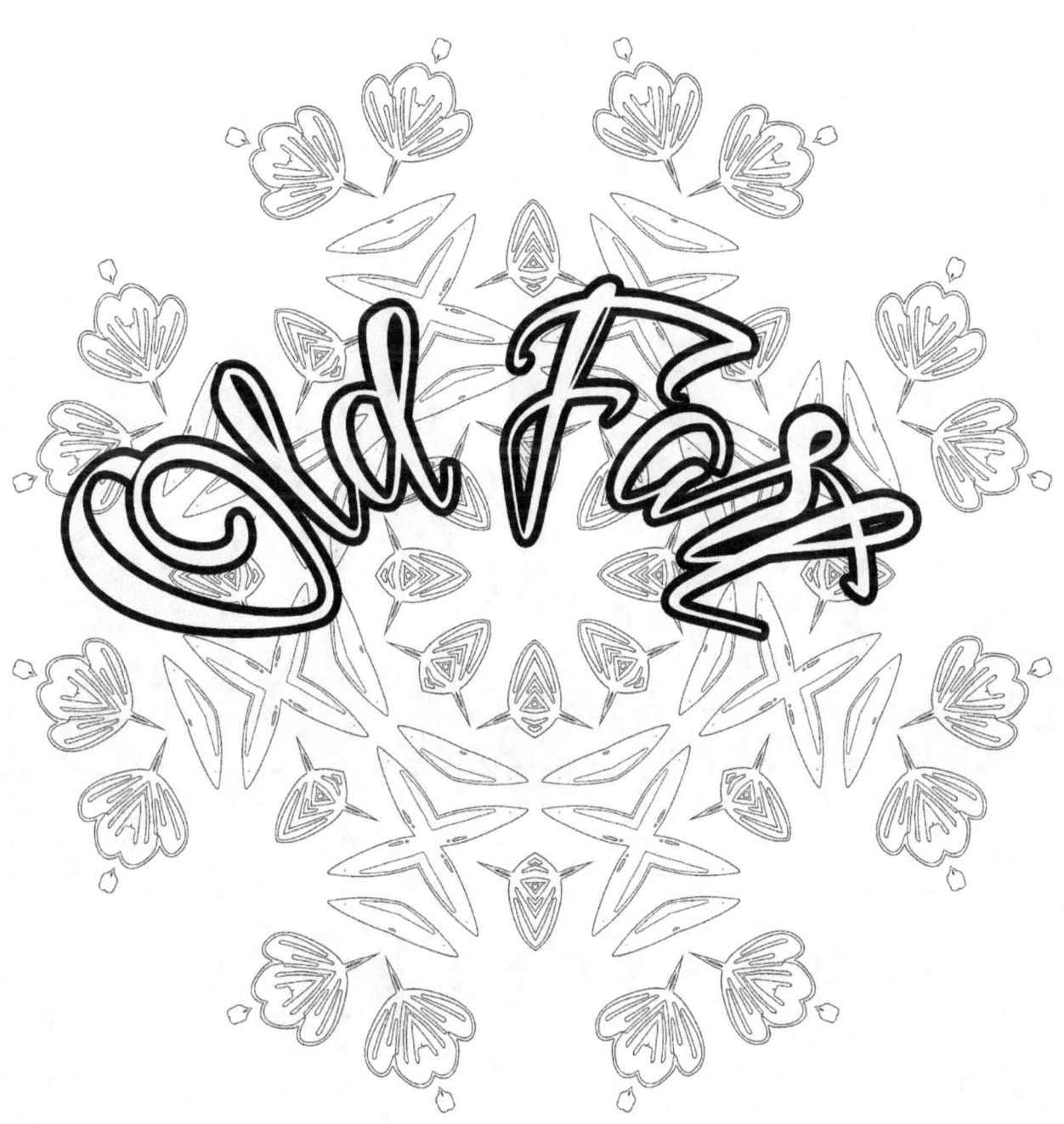

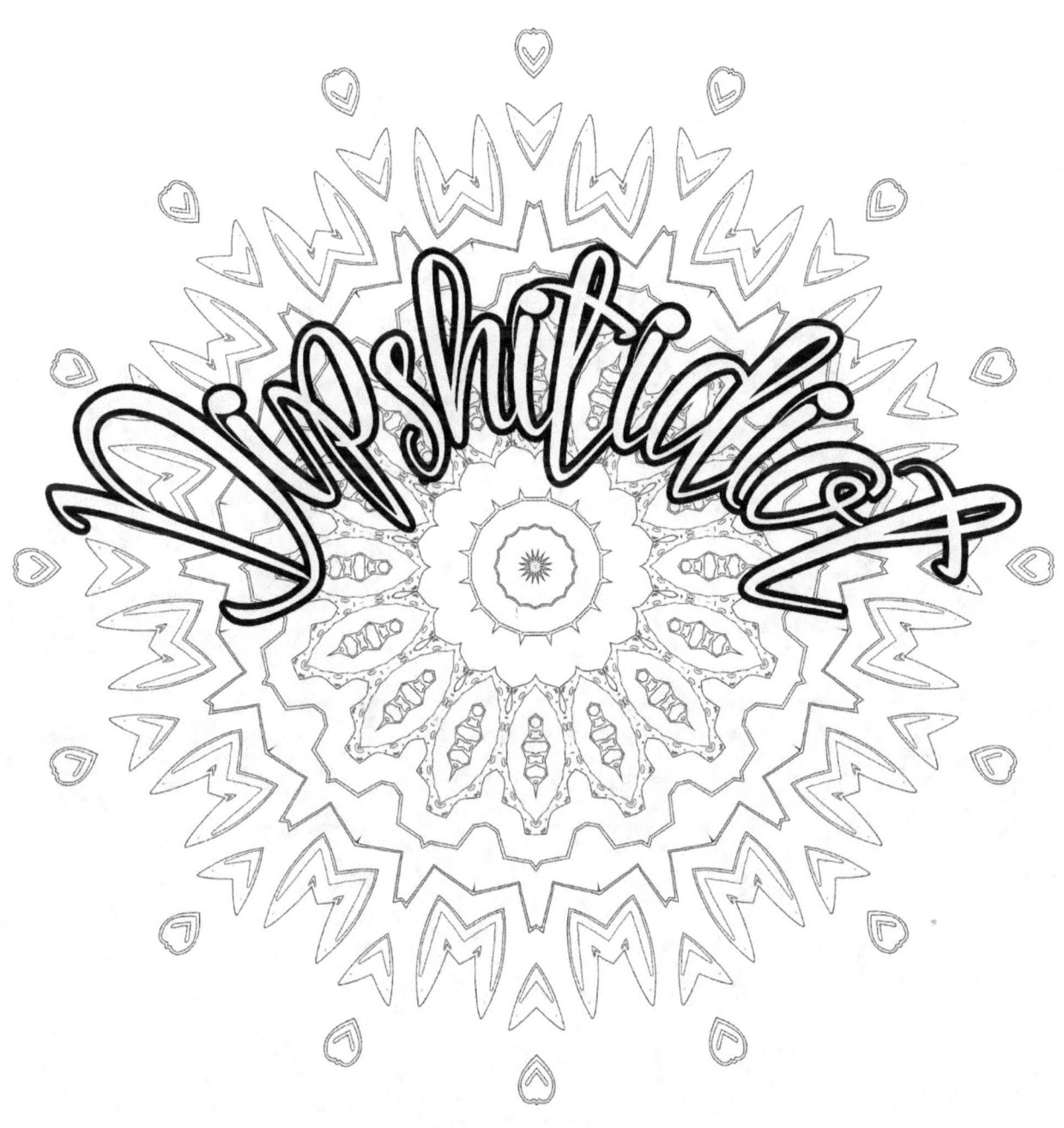

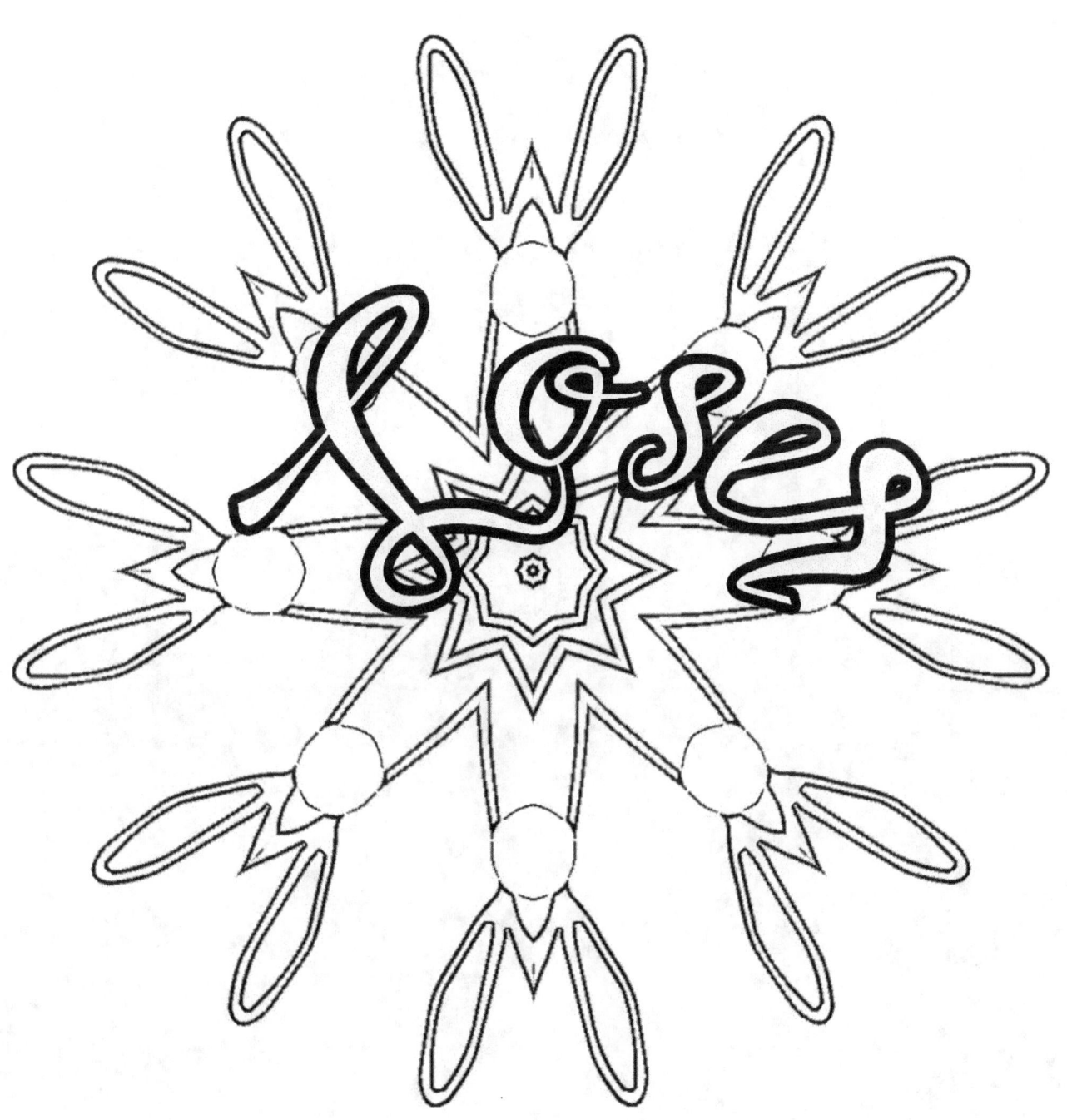

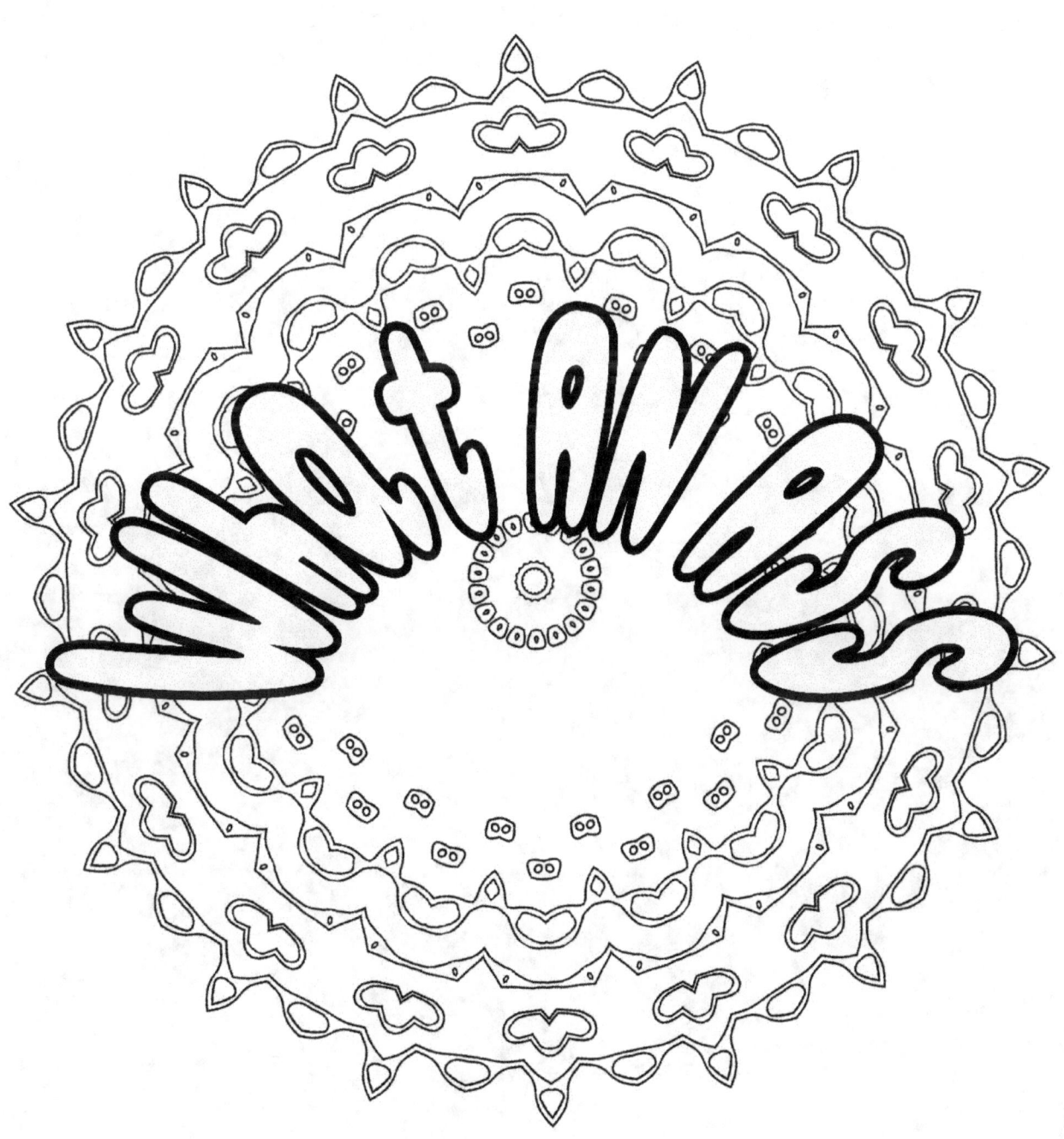

www.ingramcontent.com/pod-product-compliance
Lightning Source LLC
Chambersburg PA
CBHW081747170526
45167CB00009B/3949